Cloudy

with a

Chance of Manna

God's Promises are True. Every Time, All the Time

Jim Gribnitz

WestBow Press books may be ordered through booksellers or by contacting:

WestBow Press
A Division of Thomas Nelson & Zondervan
1663 Liberty Drive
Bloomington, IN 47403
www.westbowpress.com
1 (866) 928-1240

Because of the dynamic nature of the Internet, any web addresses or links contained in this book may have changed since publication and may no longer be valid. The views expressed in this work are solely those of the author and do not necessarily reflect the views of the publisher, and the publisher hereby disclaims any responsibility for them.

Any people depicted in stock imagery provided by Thinkstock are models, and such images are being used for illustrative purposes only.
Certain stock imagery © Thinkstock.

ISBN: 978-1-5127-1914-7 (sc)
ISBN: 978-1-5127-1913-0 (e)

Library of Congress Control Number: 2015918541

Print information available on the last page.

WestBow Press rev. date: 04/07/2016

This book is dedicated to:

The boys and girls of the Church of Jesus Christ.
You are not only the Church of tomorrow.
You are the Church of today.

Notes for parents:

1. This is an opportunity to make sure your kid knows this is inspired by a TRUE story as seen through the eyes of a little boy.

2. Instead of just telling them the story from a few thousand years ago, use it as a chance to talk about how God's promises are still true "every time, all the time"...even today!

3. A simple closing prayer can be "thank You God, that Your promises are always true. Every time, all the time."

It had been two months since a man named Moses saved us from some really hard times we were having in the country of Egypt. I wasn't really sure who Moses was at first, but I saw him do miraculous, incredible things and he told all of us that he could help us with power that God gave him!

We all had to work very hard and were very poor in Egypt. It made us really sad. Then, Moses saved my family and all of God's people from being slaves! You should have seen how happy we were when Moses freed us!

Another time, there was a lake of water that was too bitter to drink from, and we were all really thirsty. God showed Moses a tree he could use that would clean the water. It was so amazing! It was clear God wanted everyone to see He was using Moses to help us and Moses was not doing all these miracles by himself.

Moses trusted God and so God was with him. We trusted Moses, even though
we had to wander and wander and wander for a long time to get the land we
had been promised.

Even though my family did, not everyone trusted God or Moses all the time. Some people even quit trusting Moses and had to keep being reminded that God was in charge. It's like they forgot the answer to the question: "Does God really keep His promises?"

One day while we were walking, we became very hungry, but the adults hadn't packed any food because it would be too heavy to carry on our long walk. I was worried.... would God take care of us? Would He feed us?

I looked around and saw no trees with fruit to eat. There weren't any fields that grew wheat for bread or vegetables for us either!

My dad wasn't worried though. He had been told what would happen and he told us that God promised that bread would rain down from heaven every day. My dad told me, "Son, God's promises are true. Every time, all the time."

Bread would fall from heaven? It did seem a little hard to believe. Some of the men even laughed, but my mom and dad did not. My parents reminded the men who were laughing what Moses had taught them such a long time ago; God made the land we are walking on, the sun in the sky, the stars at night, the water, everything! Even us! If He can do all those incredible things, surely He can do something like give us food from heaven.

I went to bed, thinking. This sounded like a pretend story - food coming down from heaven? But could it be true? Could God's promise really be trusted? Every time, all the time?

I woke up late the next morning, even though I had planned to get up early. I ran to go look outside, but my Mom stopped me.

"Breakfast?" she said, smiling.
Yes! God did what He promised He would do!

I looked at how much we had. It wasn't very much. I thought "no way will this be enough!"

I ate slowly and wanted to leave enough for my parents. I ate slowly and carefully, mulling over each bite in my mouth until I was full. It was the strangest thing. I had exactly the right amount. Not too much. Not too little. Just right.

"Wow!" I thought. "Maybe God's promises *can* be trusted every time all the time???"

I walked outside, looked up, and wondered... "What if it doesn't come back tomorrow?"

Then a little speck of white caught my eye. Could it be? Yes! A bunch of manna was still laying around on the ground. I had a great idea. I could save some for our family, just in case it doesn't work tomorrow.

I started to collect it. Not too much... Just enough for me and my family – just in case the food didn't come tomorrow like God said it would.

"Put that down, son," said my dad.

"But, Dad...all the other families are picking it up!"

(I waved my hand, pointing to the other families scrambling to pick up what was left and hide it.)

"That way they are sure to have enough for tomorrow, too!"

"We don't need to do that."

"Why?"

"God promised that He will provide and God's promises can be trusted. Every time, all the time." Said my dad.

I watched the others still scooping up armloads and hiding it in jars. "Man", I thought. "They will have plenty of food for weeks if God doesn't keep His promise tomorrow."

I looked at my dad. I looked back at my arms full of bread. And...plunk, plunk, plunk... I let my bread fall back to the ground. I was sad, but I closed my eyes and said "God's promises can be trusted - every time, all the time."

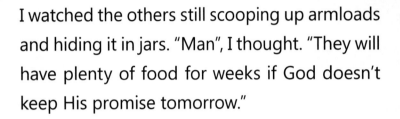

The next morning I did get up early- before my parents. I walked to the corner of our little house and went to fling open the door. I paused. I got nervous. What if there was no food? What if God has forgotten about us? What if He broke His promise? What would we eat? (I sure was hungry.)

I took a deep breath and thought to myself, "God's promises can be trusted. Every time, all the time." I slowly peered outside.

More food! Lots of it! God had provided just like He promised He would!

Everyone was so happy! Everyone except those who had gathered food the night before to save it. They were all holding their noses. It looked like all the bread they had hidden had gotten all yucky and spoiled overnight. It stunk real badly and they couldn't eat any of it! We would have to trust God's promises each and every day.

And we did.... for 40 years!

Time passed, I grew up, and had a family of my own. I watched Moses grow old and then one day he was not with us anymore. So God provided someone else to lead us: a man named Joshua.

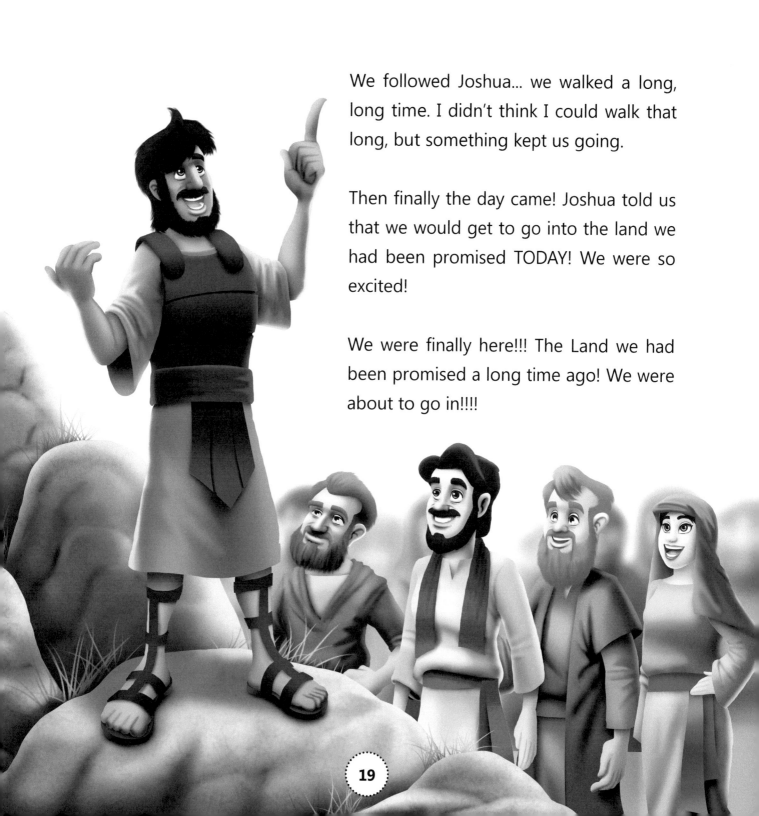

We followed Joshua... we walked a long, long time. I didn't think I could walk that long, but something kept us going.

Then finally the day came! Joshua told us that we would get to go into the land we had been promised TODAY! We were so excited!

We were finally here!!! The Land we had been promised a long time ago! We were about to go in!!!!

I was full of excitement, because this was the land that God had promised us!

Then, I felt a little tug at my sleeve.

"Dad?" My son asked.
"Yes, son?"

"I hear people talking about some really big people in the land. Should we be scared? I know God said He would give us this land, but can He do that Daddy?"

I got on my knee and said, "Son, we will enter the land today."

"How can we be sure, Daddy?"

"Because I know for sure that God's promises are true."

"Every time, all the time."

Printed in the United States
by Baker & Taylor Publisher Services